CLOSER LOOK AT

RIVERS
& LAKES

Sarah Levete

COPPER BEECH BOOKS
Brookfield, Connecticut

© Aladdin Books Ltd 1998
Designed and produced by
Aladdin Books Ltd
28 Percy Street
London W1P 0LD

*First published in the United States
in 1999 by*
Copper Beech Books,
an imprint of
The Millbrook Press
2 Old New Milford Road
Brookfield, Connecticut 06804

Editor
Michael Flaherty

Designer
Jeff Gurney

Picture Research
Brooks Krikler Research

Front cover illustration
Gary Edgar-Hyde

Illustrators
Ron Hayward and Associates,
Mike Saunders, Simon Tegg,
Aziz Khan, Michaela Stewart,
Jeff Gurney, John Rignall,
Norman Weaver, Ian Moores,
David Burroughs, Ken Stott — B.L. Kearley

Certain illustrations have appeared in
earlier books created by Aladdin Books.

Consultant
Cally Hall

Cataloging-in-Publication Data is on file at the
Library of Congress.

ISBN 0-7613-0904-7 (lib. bdg.)

5 4 3 2 1

CONTENTS

4. Introduction
6. River sources
8. Life of a river
10. Life of a lake
12. Shaping the landscape
14. Plants and wildlife
16. Going underground
18. River features
20. Water for life
22. Trade and shipping
24. Too wet, too dry
26. Pollution alert
28. Looking to the future
30. Fascinating facts
31. Glossary
32. Index

INTRODUCTION

Over millions of years, rivers and lakes have shaped our landscape and provided a source of fresh water, which is essential for animal and plant life. Fresh water is a vital resource that we need to protect from the damaging effects of pollution. From homes to factories, communities depend on rivers and lakes, but they can also be devastated by them. A river that bursts its banks or a lake that floods can destroy anything and everything in its path.

River sources

Rivers can be fed by many different sources. The longest river in the world, the Nile River in Africa, begins as two separate rivers — the White Nile and the Blue Nile. The source of the White Nile is Lake Victoria (above) in eastern Africa. It is the second largest freshwater lake in the world and straddles the borders of Uganda, Kenya, and Tanzania. As it flows north to the Mediterranean Sea, the White Nile is joined by the Blue Nile at Khartoum in the Sudan. The Blue Nile has its source in the mountains of Ethiopia, where it is fed by heavy seasonal rains.

A river is a flow of fresh water that cuts out a channel in the ground. A river can begin as a tiny trickle of water high up in the mountains. As it flows downward, the beginning, or source, of the river is fed with more water from streams, other rivers, and rainfall. The most common river sources are melting glaciers and springs. Rivers eventually empty into other rivers, lakes, or the sea.

RIVER

Surface water

Permeable rock

Impermeable rock

Springs

Ground water

SPRINGING UP

When it rains over hills and mountains (above), some of the water is absorbed by plants, some runs over the land into rivers (runoff), and some seeps underground into permeable rocks, which hold water like a sponge (groundwater). When groundwater meets impermeable rock, which doesn't let water through, the water is forced to spread outward until it comes out of the ground as a spring — a river source.

ON CLOSER INSPECTION
– *Streaming along*
Pulled downward by gravity, river sources meet other sources to form streams (right). Streams that flow from river sources are called the headwaters. During a stream's course, other surface water is added until the stream becomes a river.

SOURCES

The beginning, or head, of a glacier

Rivers of ice
A valley glacier (right) begins with snowfall in a hollow, high in the mountains. Cold air turns the snow to ice and, after thousands of years, the ice builds up to form a glacier. Eventually the ice spills out of the hollow, and its own weight causes it to slide downward. Lower down the mountainside, the ice may begin to melt. A melting glacier can become the source of a river.

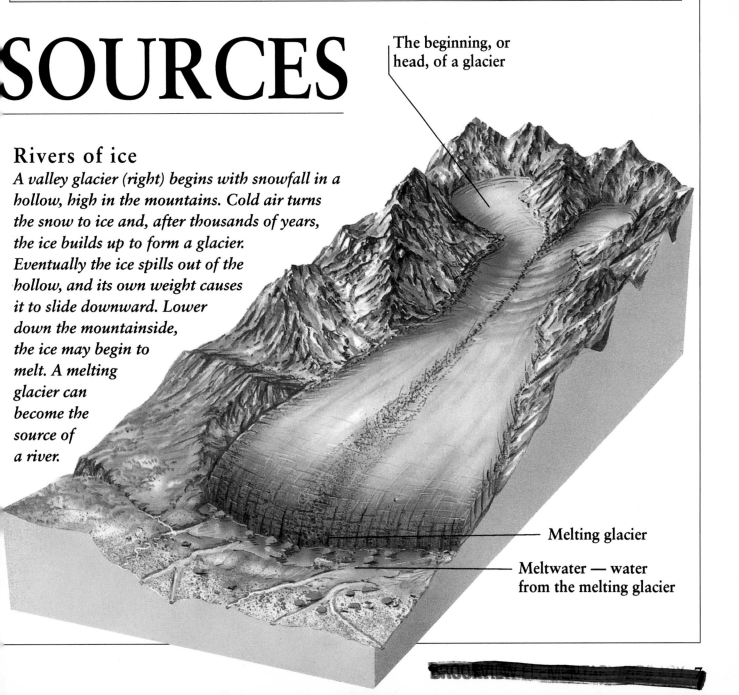

Melting glacier

Meltwater — water from the melting glacier

A river passes through many different stages in its lifetime. Because it is constantly moving and passing through new landscapes, the river's character changes between its source and mouth. Its shape, speed, and load (what it carries) all depend on the land and rocks through which it flows. In turn, the river alters the landscape around it.

Open wide!

As the river comes to the end of its course, it forms a broad, shallow mouth (above) as its waters empty into a lake or the sea.

LIFE OF A

THE LIFE OF A RIVER

A river tends to be at its steepest in its "youth," or upper part. The water flows fastest here in most rivers and may also cut steep-sided valleys. The "mature," or middle, part of the river slows down. The river swings from side to side, or meanders, carving out a wider valley. The slower-moving water deposits debris such as gravel and mud, carried from upstream. But some fast-flowing mature rivers may still cut steep-sided valleys, such as the Rhine in Europe and the Colorado River in the United States. In its "old age," or lower part, the river winds its way slowly across a broad, flat plain. A delta may form as more material is deposited.

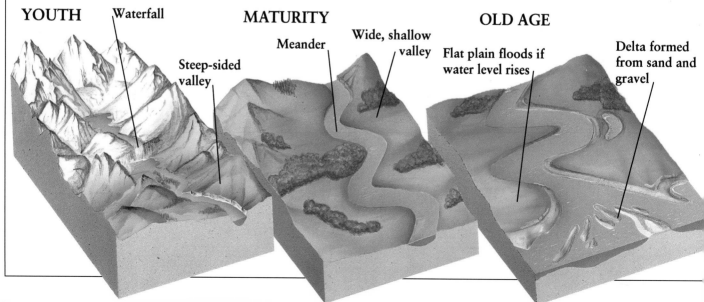

YOUTH — Waterfall

Steep-sided valley

MATURITY — Meander — Wide, shallow valley

OLD AGE — Flat plain floods if water level rises — Delta formed from sand and gravel

RIVER

THE WATER CYCLE

Water is recycled naturally. Heat from the sun turns water from oceans, rivers, and lakes into water vapor (gas). This rises into the atmosphere, where it cools and turns into water droplets, visible as clouds.

Water falls back to earth as rain or snow.

Some water sinks into the ground and may be held as groundwater for thousands of years. It eventually finds its way back into rivers, lakes, or the oceans.

Some water flows over land, forming rivers, which eventually empty into the sea.

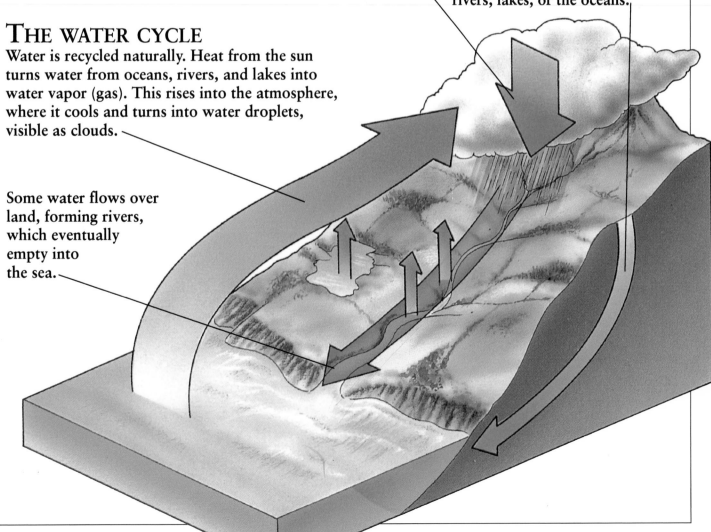

A lake is a body of still water, cut off from the sea, which stands in a hollow in the land. The water may be fresh or contain salt. Some lakes are so huge that they are called seas — the Dead Sea is, in fact, a lake. Many different forces create lakes, such as the scouring action of ice or movements of the earth's crust, creating hollows and trenches.

Crater lakes

A lake may form from rainwater, which collects in the crater resulting from a volcanic explosion (above). Some of the largest lakes are formed when huge movements of the earth's crust open up hollows, which fill with water. One of the world's oldest lakes, Lake Baikal in Russia, was formed in this way about 25 million years ago.

GLACIAL LAKES

Many lakes form in hollows created by glaciers during the Ice Age, thousands of years ago. Glaciers (see page 7) scoured out these hollows, or cirques, in the mountain rocks, which then filled with melting snow and ice. Other glacial lakes form as melting glaciers drop their load of rocks, called moraine. This forms a natural dam in the paths of rivers or streams. The lake builds up behind.

LIFE OF A

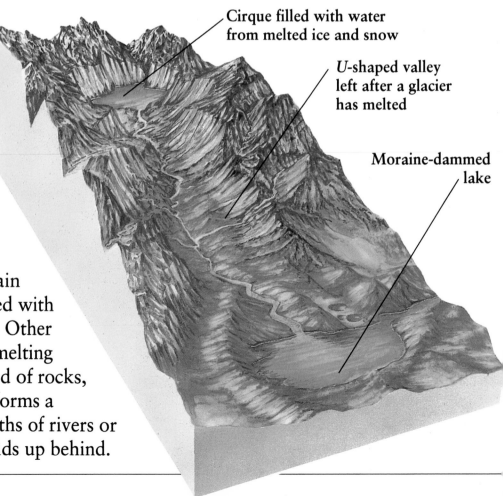

Cirque filled with water from melted ice and snow

U-shaped valley left after a glacier has melted

Moraine-dammed lake

ON CLOSER INSPECTION
– *With or without salt*

Some lakes in hot, dry climates become very salty. The salt builds up if it is not flushed away in rivers. The sun's heat evaporates the water between rainfalls, making the lake very salty. Some lakes, such as Lake Eyre in Australia, dry up, leaving a crust of salt crystals behind (right).

LAKE

Lake Geneva

Lakes can also be formed by the natural damming of a river, caused by volcanoes or ground movements, such as landslides. Lake Geneva in Switzerland (below) is the result of the natural damming of the Rhône River.

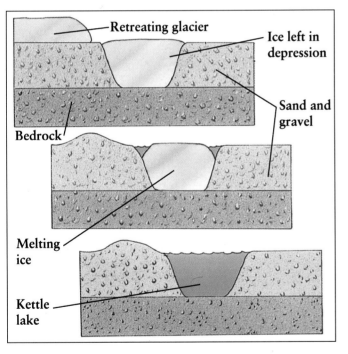

Retreating glacier

Ice left in depression

Sand and gravel

Bedrock

Melting ice

Kettle lake

KETTLE LAKES

When a glacier melts and retreats, ice may become trapped between rocks (above). When this ice melts, it forms small, circular lakes called kettle lakes.

From mountains to seas, rivers shape the land through which they travel. The strength of the water's current and the grinding motion of rocks that it carries wear away the river's banks and bed (erosion). As a river slows, it deposits rocks, sand, and mud, building up areas of new land or filling in lakes (deposition).

Valleys and canyons

In the upper part of a river, the force of the water flowing downhill is at its strongest because the slope of the channel is at its steepest. The river gradually carves out a valley that rises from the river's banks in a steep V-shape (above). In very dry climates, rocks are worn away over millions of years by the flow of a river, the wind, and the heat. This may create a canyon, which is also a deep valley, but not in the upper part of a river. Over six million years, the Colorado River, in North America, has cut through layers of rock, forming the world's largest canyon — the Grand Canyon (below).

SHAPING THE

DELTAS AND ESTUARIES

At a river mouth, the channel is broad and the current is at its slowest. The river no longer has the force to carry its load of silt and mud, which settles on the river bed, eventually clogging the channel to form new swampy land called a delta (above). Silt dropped in estuaries, where fresh river water meets salty seawater, can form salt marshes, mudflats, and lagoons.

When a river floods a plain, or a lake is taken over by plants and silt, the land becomes a marshy swamp, such as the Everglades in Florida. This swamp is fed by the Kissimmee River, and covers 2,746 sq miles (7,112 sq km).

LANDSCAPE

FLOOD PLAIN FORMATION

As the waters of a river carve a channel through the landscape, bends, or meanders, begin to appear. The water travels faster on the outside of these curves and cuts deeper into the banks. The water on the inside of the curves travels more slowly and leaves sediment on the riverbed. In this way, the meanders grow more pronounced, and a flat area builds up on the inside of each meander. When a river floods, mud and silt spread over this flat land, raising the river banks. This land becomes a flood plain. Flood plains help to prevent flood waters from spreading any farther because they store large amounts of water until the river level drops again.

A young river winds its way across the landscape, carving out a valley.

The river widens and builds up a flood plain of silt when it floods.

A mature river meanders across a wide, flat flood plain.

From tiny insects to huge hippos, rivers and lakes are home to an amazing variety of animal and plant life. All animals and plants need water, however little, to survive. Animals and plants have adapted to particular conditions in these watery environments, which show as much variation as any environment on land.

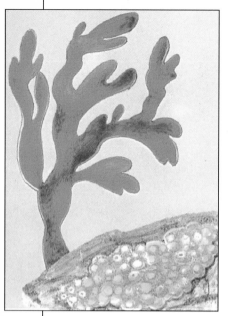

Plants
Algae (above) and green plants make their own food using the energy from sunlight. They are called producers, and they provide food for consumers, such as animals. Without water plants there would be no other water wildlife.

PLANTS AND

UP AND DOWN
Salmon hatch from eggs far upstream. They then swim downstream to the sea. Adult salmon have a strong homing instinct and recognize the scent of the river in which they hatched. After three or four years at sea, they return to their home river, struggling upstream to spawn (lay eggs). After spawning, some types of salmon die. Others return to the sea and live to spawn three or more times.

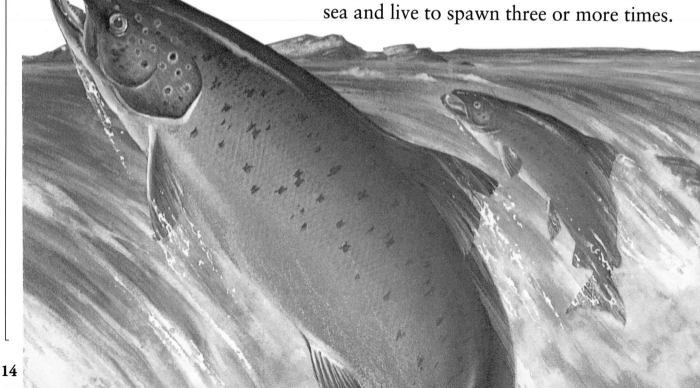

WILDLIFE

The females of many ground-nesting water birds, such as these mallard ducks (right), are drab in color, so they can blend in with their surroundings as they sit on their eggs. The males are more boldly colored, as they swim in the relative safety of the water.

WATER REPTILES

An amazing range of animals other than fish make their homes in and around the world's rivers and lakes. Reptiles, including alligators (below) and turtles, were the first true land animals. Many still live in and around rivers and lakes to benefit from the rich supply of food.

BIRDS

Many kinds of bird live in or beside water, feeding on fish and plants. Many, such as ducks (above) and geese, have developed webbing between their toes to assist in swimming. Some, such as grebes, have become such expert swimmers that they are reluctant fliers and clumsy walkers, spending almost all their lives on the water.

ivers do not only flow at ground level. They can also be found underground, especially where the rock is limestone. Some underground rivers and lakes are thousands of years old and have formed complex networks of waterways. They have also become home to strange animals that have adapted to the lightless world, such as blind cave fish of the United States.

GOING

Mites and tites

Water dripping through a limestone cave contains minerals such as calcium carbonate. Mineral deposits form spirelike shapes (above): stalactites hang from the roof; stalagmites grow up from the ground.

CAVES

Rainwater absorbs carbon dioxide, a gas in the air, and forms carbonic acid, which makes the water slightly acidic. As the rainwater seeps in between the joints or cracks in limestone rock, the acid gradually wears it away. A sinkhole forms and the river disappears underground.

A gallery, now a dry tunnel, was created when the water table was higher.

The stream emerges from a cave mouth.

Level of the water table, below which the limestone is saturated

ON CLOSER INSPECTION
– *The River Styx*

In Greek mythology, the Underworld — the kingdom of the dead — was surrounded by the River Styx. To get to the Underworld, the dead had to pay a boatman called Charon to ferry them across.

UNDERGROUND

Sinkholes

Limestone is one of the most permeable rocks — it allows water to seep into it. In areas rich in limestone rock, a stream or river flowing above ground will seep into the rock and gradually dissolve it until a hollow is formed, which can cause great damage to any surrounding buildings (below). Such holes are called sinkholes or dolines. As the river continues to flow, the doline grows bigger as more rock is dissolved. Some dolines are up to 300 feet (100 m) across.

POTHOLING

Exploring the watery world below the ground can be fascinating. Beneath our feet lies a maze of connected caves and caverns formed by lakes and rivers. Potholers (above) enjoy battling against the elements to explore these caves, but it is a dangerous sport. There is a risk of getting lost in the maze or becoming trapped by rising water levels.

Falling fast

A waterfall (below) is a vertical drop over which a river falls. It is formed by the river passing first over hard rocks, then an area of softer rock. The soft rock is worn away by the river (erosion), leaving a vertical face of the harder rock. The force of the falling water carves out a deep pool at the base of the drop called a plunge pool. Water tumbles over the Niagara Falls at 50 mph (80 km/h), eroding the rock by more than three feet (1 m) every year.

Dramatic and dangerous, waterfalls and rapids are among the world's most spectacular natural features. Along the length of their courses, rivers produce many features in the landscape. These features depend on the strength of the current and the rock types through which a river flows. Fast-flowing rivers carve away soil, sand, and soft rock, but leave harder rocks almost untouched. Slower water deposits more sediment.

RIVER

MEANDERS TO OXBOW LAKES

The bends, or meanders, in a river occur more frequently the nearer the river gets to the end of its course, where the slope is gentle and the valley is wide (see page 13). The neck of a meander narrows as the river carves away the outside edges (above). Eventually the river cuts through, sealing off the meander with sediment. This creates a crescent-shaped lake called an oxbow lake.

ON CLOSER INSPECTION
– *Sacred rivers*

The Ganges River flows for 1,550 miles (2,480 km), from the slopes of the Himalayas in India and on through Bangladesh. Many Hindus believe that the Ganges is a holy river that can cleanse the soul and body and will transport the bodies of the dead to heaven.

FEATURES

RAPIDS

Often found near waterfalls and in the upper parts of rivers, rapids occur where fast-flowing, shallow water becomes churned up as it hurtles over boulders and hard rock ledges (below). Ledges of hard rock are exposed when the surrounding soft rock is worn away. Sometimes a series of rapids occur along a stretch of water. These are known as cataracts. Taking a boat over rapids is very dangerous, but some people enjoy the challenge of trying to negotiate the rapids in canoes or rafts.

BRAIDING AND EYOTS

Braided rivers have many criss-crossing channels like braids in hair. Braiding occurs in rivers that travel down steep slopes over gravel or sand beds. The coarse sediment is loose, but the water cannot carry it away. The river threads its way around gravel bars and small islands called eyots. Where rivers flow sluggishly, fine sediment may also build up to form eyots (above).

rom generating electricity to supplying faucets in our homes, water is a precious resource. Only 3 percent of the world's water is fresh water. Most of this is locked in glaciers and polar ice. Rivers and lakes hold less than 0.02 percent of the world's water, and it is this that supplies most of our needs.

Reservoirs

Many natural lakes, like this small mountain lake, or tarn, in Wales (above), are used as reservoirs. The tarn is fed by rainwater, and the water must be filtered and purified before it is safe to drink.

WATER FOR

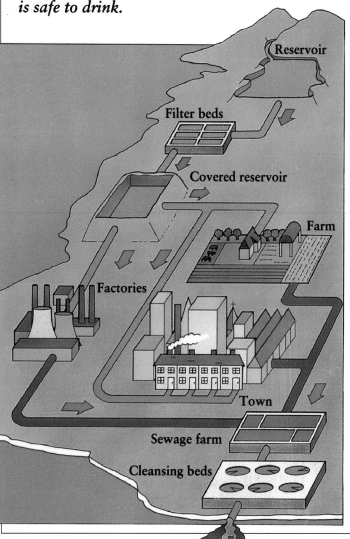

Reservoir

Filter beds

Covered reservoir

Farm

Factories

Town

Sewage farm

Cleansing beds

WATER TO USE

The water that we drink, use for washing, or even just flushing the toilet has to be treated to make it clean for everyday use. The water is first filtered to remove debris and then purified to destroy disease-carrying bacteria. When it has been treated, the water flows to a covered reservoir, or pumping station. Reservoirs are storage areas for water used to ensure a constant supply, especially in dry seasons. From the reservoir, the water is pumped along a system of underground pipes, known as the water main. This supplies water to homes and factories. The water is pumped with such force, or pressure, that it can reach every faucet. Waste water is carried away in sewers to sewage plants, where it is then cleaned before being returned to rivers.

From sailing to fishing, people all over the world enjoy splashing around in the water. However, whenever you are near or on a river or lake, always be careful. It is possible to drown in even shallow and calm water.

LIFE

IRRIGATION
Where there is not enough rainfall to meet agricultural needs, water can be channeled from rivers and lakes, through canals and ditches. This is called irrigation. This sprinkler irrigation system on wheels (below) moves across a field spraying crops with a fine mist of water.

WORKING WATER
The force of falling water or water moving downhill can be used to run machines that generate electricity. Artificial dams, such as El Chicon in Argentina (above), cause a large body of water to collect that produces the pressure needed to drive the turbines and electrical generators. Sluice gates control the water flow from the dam along narrowing tunnels to turbines in the powerhouse below the dam. The movement of the water turns the turbines and generators, which create an electrical current as they rotate. The electrical current is carried by cables to pylons carrying the power supply.

21

Flooding to grow

Some rivers flood at the same time every year. Floods are not always bad news. Flood waters leave the land rich with organic and mineral deposits, making it fertile and ideal for growing crops. On the delta plains of the Mekong River in Vietnam and the Ganges River in India, farmers build protective walls to keep the paddy fields permanently flooded. This ensures a successful rice crop.

The new fertile deposits from annual flooding allow crops to be grown every year without exhausting the soil.

The first great civilizations developed and prospered in river valleys such as the Nile Valley of Egypt and the Indus Valley of India and Pakistan. Rivers supply necessary water for irrigation, and flood waters deposit nutrient-rich sediment that makes the earth fertile. Towns and cities have often developed around rivers as many communities rely on agriculture for food. Rivers are also necessary for transporting crops to markets in different towns.

TRADE AND

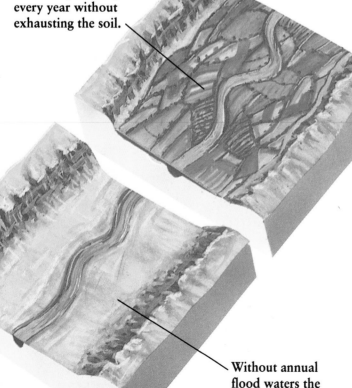

Without annual flood waters the land would be too dry to grow crops.

TRANSPORTATION

Freighters, barges and boats transport goods along the world's rivers and across its lakes. The first boats were probably log canoes or rafts. The ancient Egyptians were sailing rafts on the Nile in 5000 B.C. Today's freighters and container ships are enormous steel constructions (above).

The first bridges were probably logs or vines laid across streams and rivers. The Babylonians built the first bridge recorded in history in about 2200 B.C. Today, high-tech bridges are designed and made using the latest materials and technological skills, such as this bridge (right), which crosses a dock along the Thames River in London, England.

SHIPPING

Locks

As the steepness of the slope changes along a canal or river, water-filled chambers called locks are used to raise or lower ships. The Gatun Lock along the Panama Canal (below) consists of three pairs of concrete chambers that raise or lower ships 85 feet (26 m) as they pass to or from the Gatun Lake from either the Atlantic or the Pacific oceans.

CANALS

In the 1880s, to meet the demands of trade, many rivers and lakes were channeled into artifical waterways called canals (above). Canals are often long and straight — ideal for heavy ships carrying tons of cargo. Canals are constructed to connect major shipping routes to each other.

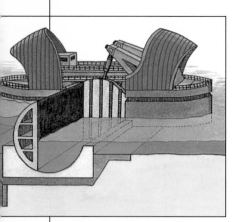

ivers are an essential water source, but they can be unpredictable. Communities that depend on rivers can also be destroyed by them. If the weather becomes too dry, the water dries up; too wet, and there is danger of flooding. When the Yellow River in China overflowed in 1887, over two million people died and two thousand towns and cities were destroyed.

TOO WET,

Thames Barrier

Storms can cause the sea level to rise. Seawater then surges up river mouths. Water may spill over the banks, flooding the land. Flood barriers are built near estuaries to prevent flooding. The gates of the Thames Flood Barrier (above) are closed to seal off the river estuary, so that the sea does not flood London.

Gravity dam

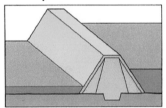

Buttress dam

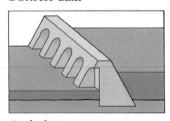

Arch dam

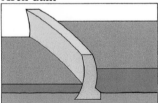

Cantilever dam

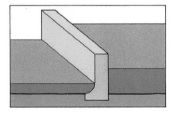

ALL DAMMED UP

A dam is a barrier across a river that halts the flow of water. It helps prevent flooding and provides a reservoir of water. The type of dam (left) used depends on the local geography. A gravity dam, made of solid stone, holds the water through its sheer size and weight. A buttress dam, supported from behind the dam face, is used when a long, straight dam is needed. An arch dam is built over high-banked rivers or across steep-sided gorges. Cantilever dams have thin concrete walls embedded with heavy metal rods. But water is heavy. If a dam bursts, the effects are catastrophic.

Dried up

Long periods with little rainfall cause droughts. Rivers and lakes dry up and plants wither as the soil becomes parched and cracked (above). This can leave communities without food or essential water.

Flooding across Eastern Europe in 1997, particularly in Poland and eastern Germany (right), devastated large areas when the Odane River burst its banks. Such flooding breaks communication and power lines and may rupture gas mains, causing fires. It will take many years and millions of dollars to repair the damage.

TOO DRY

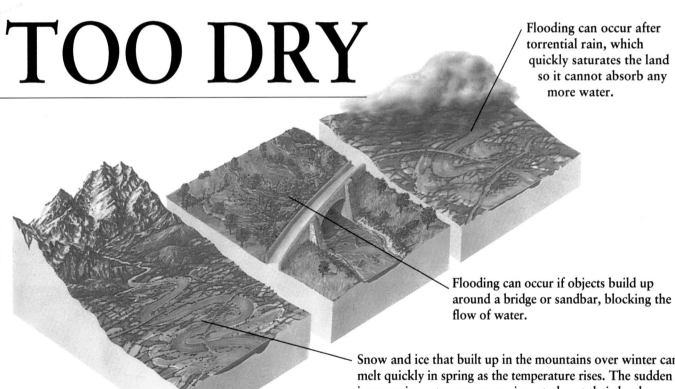

Flooding can occur after torrential rain, which quickly saturates the land so it cannot absorb any more water.

Flooding can occur if objects build up around a bridge or sandbar, blocking the flow of water.

Snow and ice that built up in the mountains over winter can melt quickly in spring as the temperature rises. The sudden increase in water can cause rivers to burst their banks.

FLOODING

In temperate or mild climates, many rivers flood their banks at least once a year. The warmer weather of spring melts snow and ice from surrounding mountains, which results in a flow of water too great for the ground to absorb. In tropical climates, short but heavy periods of rainfall can also cause floods. In southern Asia, the monsoon winds bring heavy rainfall, which often causes the rivers to flood.

Polluting poisons

When waste is released into water, the oxygen in the water tries to break down the pollutants. This deprives animal and plant life of vital oxygen supplies. Chemical wastes added to the water may cause algae to grow rapidly, covering the water with a thick green layer (below). This can choke a river and upset the natural balance of life in the water and on land.

uch time and money is spent trying to maintain a constant supply of fresh water through irrigation or building dams and reservoirs. In developed countries, attention is now being given to keeping rivers, lakes, and seas free of industrial and human pollutants. In the poorer developing countries, there often isn't the money available to spend on such measures.

POLLUTION

CAUSES OF POLLUTION

In the modern world, water is polluted in many ways through lack of care (right). Oil tankers and refineries leak oil into the sea. Factories have been discharging untreated waste into rivers for over a century. Fertilizers and pesticides seep into water supplies. Factory chimneys and car exhausts pump poisonous gases into the air, causing acid rain. Many countries now have laws to control this, but damage continues. Pollution destroys the balance of nature, which we all rely on for our survival.

ON CLOSER INSPECTION
– *Global warming*

Some scientists believe the earth's temperature is increasing due to rising levels of certain gases in the atmosphere caused by pollution. The effects on the climate may vary in different places. Some places may already be getting drier, causing rivers to dry up, such as the Frome River (right) in England.

ALERT

ACID LAKE

Pollutants in the air increase the natural acidity of rain. As this rain falls into rivers and lakes, it makes the water more acidic. This affects the health of plants and insects that live in and around the water (below), and disrupts the food chain. The food chain is the natural process by which different forms of life — from the smallest bacteria to humans — rely on each other as a source of food in a continual cycle. Disrupting this natural order has a ripple effect, depriving insects, fish, birds, and other animals, including humans, of their natural food sources.

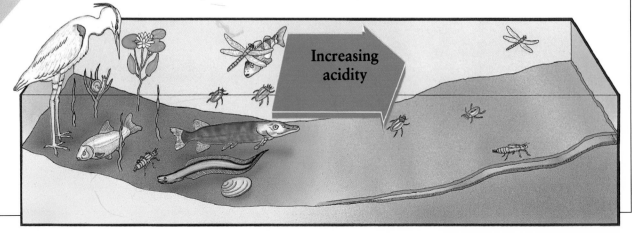

HEALTHY LAKE
Contains a wide variety of wildlife.

ACID LAKE
Very few species can survive the increase in acidity.

Increasing acidity

Rivers and lakes supply us with water and are also home for wildlife. The amount of water we take from them has an effect on the environment. Rivers often flow through more than one country. Countries don't always agree on how best to manage the waterways to ensure supplies for now and the future, and to protect the environment.

LOOKING TO

Water in dispute

Since civilizations began, people have fought over water. As we increase our usage of this vital resource, and climatic changes affect available supplies, water may become the cause of future conflict — wars and international disputes may be fought over water supplies rather than land. In 1956, war almost broke out when President Nasser of Egypt seized control of the Suez Canal, which links the Mediterranean and Red seas. The Suez Canal is an important industrial waterway. For the sake of world peace, control of such vital waterways is of international importance.

SUPPLY AND DEMAND

More than 70 percent of the earth is covered with water. Many scientists believe that pollution is affecting the climate, resulting in less rainfall in many places to feed rivers and lakes. Most of the water used in homes and industry can be cleaned and returned to rivers to be reused. But water used for irrigation is not returned to rivers in this way. It is returned through the water cycle. In Australia where the climate is dry, 74 percent of water is used for irrigation.

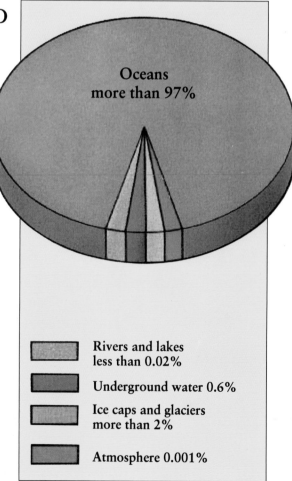

Oceans more than 97%

Rivers and lakes less than 0.02%

Underground water 0.6%

Ice caps and glaciers more than 2%

Atmosphere 0.001%

Plans for a 2,000-mile (3,000-km) waterway network joining the Tocantin and Araguaia rivers in the Amazon will benefit industry, but will seriously affect the six thousand Indians in the area. They will have to move from their ancestral home and try to forge a new life elsewhere.

THE FUTURE

The Challenges
In developed countries, each person uses about 69 gallons (260 l) of water a day. Of that figure, 2.6 gallons (10 l) are used to flush the toilet, 21 gallons (80 l) to take a bath, or 8 gallons (30 l) for a shower. Surprisingly, 115 gallons (435 l) are needed to grow enough wheat to bake a loaf of bread (below). In many developing countries, pollution control is expensive, and many people still use untreated water, which carries many harmful bacteria. Water-related diseases kill twenty-five thousand children every day. To prevent water shortages and pollution, we need to improve the care of our rivers and lakes, and find cheaper, more efficient ways of desalinating (removing salt from) seawater.

WATER WASTAGE
In homes and industries, water seems plentiful. Because fresh water is constantly available, pumped directly into our homes, it is easy to allow fresh water to be wasted without realizing it, such as by keeping the faucet running while brushing our teeth. Water systems need to be well-maintained and free of

leaks (left) to cut down on wastage. A single leaking faucet could waste the equivalent of four hundred bathtubs of water a year. It can take many years for lost water to find its way back to a river.

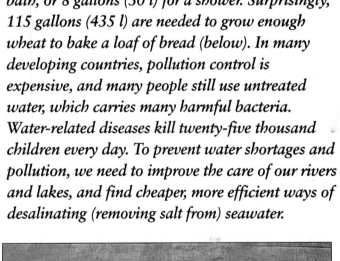

The walls of the Grand Canyon are like a cross-section through time.

The Angel Falls in Venezuela have a total drop of 3,212 feet (979 m) and are the world's highest waterfall.

The Amazon River in South America carries more water than any other river and more than the Mississippi, the Nile, and the Yangtze together. It carries one fifth of the world's fresh water.

Europe's longest river is the Volga. It flows for 2,207 miles (3,531 km) into the Caspian Sea.

The Caspian Sea is the world's largest natural lake, covering an area of 143,600 sq miles (372,000 sq km).

The Yangtze River in China usually deposits 33 million gallons of water into the sea per second. When it floods, that amount of water can double. The river can flood over 70,000 sq miles (180,000 sq km).

FASCINATING FACTS

The Grand Canyon (above) in Arizona is 217 miles (347 km) long, 4 to 18 miles (6 to 28 km) wide and 1 mile (1.6 km) deep. Carved out of the rock by the Colorado River, it is the largest land gorge in the world.

The water of the Niagara Falls on the U.S.-Canadian border (below) drops at 50 mph (80 km/h). The falls are now 7 miles (11 km) farther up river through erosion than when they began about 12,000 years ago.

The deep, dark waters of Loch Ness may be home to an ancient monster.

The Nile River flows for 4,145 miles (6,670 km) through northeast Africa. It is the world's longest river.

The world's lowest lake is the Dead Sea, between Israel and Jordan in southwestern Asia. It lies 1,285 feet (392 m) below sea level. It is nine times saltier than the sea.

Loch Ness in Scotland holds more water than any other British lake, with a volume of 2.6 billion cubic feet.

The longest river in the United States is the Mississippi. It is 2,350 miles (3,800 km) long. Dredgers are used to remove the silt that threaten to block the shallow water.

Niagara Falls formed after the last Ice Age.

Acid rain Rain that is more acidic than normal because of the chemicals from car exhausts and industry.

Braiding Commonly occurs where the river threads its way around sand and gravel bars, forming a pattern like braided hair.

Canal An artificial waterway.

Delta The fan-shaped area around a river mouth made of sediment that often splits the river into many smaller channels.

Erosion The wearing away of land by the action of water, wind, and ice.

Estuary When a river mouth opens into the sea, the part of the river where fresh water mixes with salt water.

Eyot Also spelled *ait*, it is a small island, especially one found in a river.

Flood plain A broad, flat area on either side of the lower course of a river that is covered with sediment from the river each time it floods.

Glacier A mass of ice formed on high ground by the buildup of snow.

Global warming A rise in the earth's temperature that may be caused by an increase in carbon dioxide and other greenhouse gases that trap heat from the sun in the earth's atmosphere.

Groundwater The water found in the soil and in cracks and pores in underground rocks.

Hydroelectric power Electricity generated by turbines that are driven by flowing water.

Irrigation Bringing water to dry areas through artificial channels, pipes, or sprinklers in order to water crops.

Loch The Scots Gaelic word for *lake*.

Lock A chamber with gates at either end built into a river or canal channel. The water level in the chamber can be changed to raise or lower ships as they pass up- or downstream.

Meander A natural bend in a river, usually occurring in the middle course.

Permeable Of rock, allowing water to pass through.

GLOSSARY

Reservoir A large natural or artificial lake used to store water for drinking and other day-to-day needs, industry, farming, and making electricity.

Runoff Rainwater that runs over land away from where it falls.

Sediment Particles of rock, sand, and soil that have been carried along and then deposited by a river.

Silt Very fine grains of sediment carried and deposited by a river.

Source The origin of a river, whether it be a spring, a mountain lake, or a melting glacier.

Tributary A river or stream that flows into a larger river or lake.

Turbine A row of blades around a shaft that may be turned by water, steam, or other gases.

Water table The level at which the ground is saturated, or full, of water.

INDEX

acid rain 26, 27, 31
Angel Falls 30
animals 14, 15, 26

bacteria 20, 27, 29
banks 13, 25
birds 15
braiding 19, 31

canals 21, 23, 31
  Panama Canal 23
  Suez Canal 28

Grand Canyon 12, 30
gravel 8, 11, 19, 31
groundwater 6, 31

hydroelectric power 31

ice 7, 10, 11, 20, 25, 31
industry 28, 29, 30, 31
irrigation 21, 22, 26, 28, 31

Niagara Falls 18, 30

oxbow lakes 18

plants 6, 13, 14–15, 19, 24, 26, 27
pollution 4, 26, 27, 28, 29

rain 6, 9, 11, 16, 21, 24, 25, 28, 31
rapids 18, 19
reservoirs 20, 24, 26, 31
rivers 4, 6, 7, 8, 9, 12, 16, 20, 22, 23, 25, 26, 27, 28, 29
  Amazon 29, 30
  Colorado 12, 30
  Frome 27
  Ganges 18, 22
  Mississippi 9, 30
  Nile 6, 22, 30
  Odane 25
  Rhône 11
  Styx 17
  Thames 23
  Volga 30
  Yangtze 30
  Yellow 24
rocks 6, 8, 10, 12, 16, 17, 18, 30, 31
  impermeable 6
  permeable 6, 31
run-off 6, 31

salt 10, 11, 12, 29, 30
sand 8, 11, 12, 18, 19, 25, 31
seas 6, 8, 9, 10, 24, 26, 29, 30
  Caspian Sea 30
  Mediterranean Sea 6, 28
  Red Sea 28
sediment 18, 19, 22, 31
silt 12, 13, 30, 31
sinkholes 17

snow 7, 9, 10, 25, 31
sources 6–7, 31
springs 6, 31
streams 6, 7, 10, 16, 23, 31
swamps 13

tarns 20
Thames Barrier 23
turbines 21, 31

valleys 7, 8, 10, 12, 13, 18
volcanoes 10

water 6, 7, 8, 9, 12, 20, 24, 26, 27, 29
  cycle 31
  meltwater 7
  rain 10, 16, 31
  sea 12, 24, 29
  surface 6, 7
  table 16, 31
  vapor 9
waterfalls 8, 18, 19, 30
wildlife 13, 14–15, 27

carbon dioxide 16, 31
cataracts 19
cirques 10
climate 12, 25

dams 10, 21, 24, 26
debris 11
deltas 8, 12, 22, 31
droughts 24

erosion 12, 18, 30, 31
estuaries 12, 24, 31
Everglades 13
eyots 18, 19, 31

factories 4, 20, 26
farms 20
fish 15, 16, 27
floods 4, 13, 22, 24, 30, 31
flood plains 13, 31
fresh water 4, 6, 28, 29, 30

glaciers 6, 7, 10, 11, 20, 31
global warming 27, 31

lakes 4, 6, 7, 8, 9, 10, 16, 20, 22, 26, 27, 28, 29, 30
  Dead Sea 10, 30
  Gatun Lake 23
  kettle lakes 11
  Lake Baikal 10
  Lake Eyre 11
  Lake Geneva 11
  Lake Victoria 6
  Loch Ness 15
landslides 11
limestone 16, 17
loads 8, 10
locks 23, 31

marshes 12, 13
meanders 8, 13, 18, 31
monsoons 25
monsters 15, 30
moraine 10
mountains 6, 7, 8, 19, 25
mouths, river 8
mud 12, 13, 30
mudflats 12

Photo credits

Abbreviations:
t-top, m-middle,
b-bottom, r-right, l-left.

Pages 1, 2-3, 5, 12
both, 18 both, 20, 21,
23m, 26, 27, 29bl &
br, & 30t — Roger
Vlitos; 6 & 10 —
Hutchinson Library;
8 — Keith Newell;
11 both, 13, & 23b —
Spectrum Colour
Library; 15, 16, 17b,
19b, 22, 25, 28, 29t,
30m & b — Frank
Spooner Pictures.